My Forever
GUARDIAN

By Kristina Jones

Illustrated by Beatriz Mello

My Forever Guardian
Subtitle | Healing with friends from the loss of a loved one
Written by Kristina Jones, Illustrated by Beatriz Mello

Title | My Forever Guardian written by Kristina Jones, Illustrated by Beatriz Mello
Description | My Forever Guardian teaches kids how to heal with friends and as a community from the loss of a loved one. This book is for children who are looking for ways to mentally and emotionally heal and transition a loved one from the physical world to being their Forever Guardian. The book also teaches children how to speak openly about healing after experiencing a death. This is the perfect book for your home, community center, church, school or counselor's office.

Media inquiries: media@guardianlane.com
Partnership inquiries: info@guardianlane.com

Hardcover ISBN : 978-1-7348142-0-0
Paperback ISBN: 978-1-7348142-1-7
EBook ISBN: 978-1-7348142-2-4

In memory of my Dad.

This book is for every child who has a Forever Guardian.
After reading, join us at guardianlane.com to heal with
a community of kids who also have Forever Guardians.

On their way to school, Sasha asked Micah, "Why are you sad, today?"
"I miss my older brother. We had fun together and now he's not here."
Micah stomped his feet a few times and kicked the curb.

Micah and Sasha are in third grade and have been friends since
kindergarten. Every day they walk back and forth to school.

"No one can replace Kevin as your brother," said Sasha.
"It is sad he's gone..."

...but now he's your Forever Guardian."

"What do you mean?" asked Micah.

"He's close to you in a different way," said Sasha. "That's what my nana says. Your new Forever Guardian watches over you and is there for you whenever you need him."

"That sounds wonderful to me!" said Micah. "I like thinking he is near me."

"Your Forever Guardian has a job to watch over you and protect you. When you feel you need a hug from him, wrap your arms around yourself and feel his embrace."

Micah stopped walking and gave himself a great big hug. Then he felt much better and not so unhappy.

"Nana also told me when you feel like crying, every tear is a sparkle of the love you have for your Forever Guardian. She said everyone loses someone they love. Then that someone becomes a Forever Guardian."

"Sometimes I get angry because I miss him so much," said Micah.

"Micah, why don't you think of a happy time with your brother? Close your eyes, and take a moment to remember him. Open your eyes when you have a warm feeling in your heart."

Micah closed his eyes and thought about playing at the park with his brother. "I don't feel angry anymore," he said. "We were swinging as high as we could, trying to touch the sky!"

15

At school they walked inside to their classroom.

After lunch and recess, Micah and Sasha and the rest of the class sat in a circle for group time.

"How does everybody feel this afternoon?" asked the teacher.

"I miss Comet, my dog, who is now my new Forever Guardian," said Robin. "I loved throwing a ball for him to catch. He ran as fast as he could and brought it back to me. I try to remember he is always with me."

Micah and Sasha quickly looked at each other in surprise. Sasha whispered to Micah, "Our friends have Forever Guardians too!"

"I have a Forever Guardian," said Jasper. "Es mi abuela. She watches over me in good times, bad times, and even when I'm scared. I feel lucky to have her close by me."

"Sometimes I hear a noise, or a whistling wind and know it is my dad, my Forever Guardian," says Kristina. "It's like little reminders for me to tell him 'I love you.'"

"Just by sharing your thoughts, you comfort one another," said the teacher. "I hope you continue to share your experiences and feelings even after our group time."

Micah, now with a big smile, and Sasha, feeling happy for her friend, skipped on their way home from school.

"I liked learning about my new Forever Guardian" said Micah. "I feel he's trying to race home with me right now!"

AUTHOR'S NOTE:

When I lost my father at the age of seven it felt like my whole world stopped. I knew my dad was ill with cancer, but I never thought he would actually pass away. Once he was gone, I found ways to connect with him through ways that I shared in the book. Through the years, my spiritual communities Agape and with my spiritual cheerleaders, my mother, my Aunt Laurel and my Aunt Silvia, I was able to strengthen my connection to my dad even more.

When I was 7, I wish I knew it was okay to speak openly with other kids about my experience. Today, with kids living in a social world, it's time to let them know it's okay to share and heal together. With the help of the best bereavement counselors, Guardianlane.com was born to help our kids socially heal. We hope you join the community!

www.ingramcontent.com/pod-product-compliance
Lightning Source LLC
Chambersburg PA
CBHW060753150426
42811CB00058B/1395